TECH GIRLS™

Careers for

TECH GIRLS IN

DIGITAL

PUBLISHING

HILLARY DODGE

Rosen
YA
New York

Published in 2019 by The Rosen Publishing Group, Inc.
29 East 21st Street, New York, NY 10010

Library of Congress Cataloging-in-Publication Data

Names: Dodge, Hillary, author.
Title: Careers for tech girls in digital publishing / Hillary Dodge.
Description: New York : Rosen Publishing, 2019. | Series: Tech girls | Includes bibliographical references and index. | Audience: Grades 7–12.
Identifiers: ISBN 9781508180142 (library bound) | ISBN 9781508180159 (pbk.)
Subjects: LCSH: Electronic publishing—Vocational guidance—Juvenile literature. | Authorship—Vocational guidance—Juvenile literature.
Classification: LCC Z286.E43 D63 2019 | DDC 070.5'797—dc23

Manufactured in the United States of America

CONTENTS

Introduction

According to the Adobe Systems Incorporated *State of Create: 2016* report, 70 percent of survey respondents said that being creative is valuable to society. The same report concludes that creators are happier at work, are valued more in the workplace, and have a stronger self-image than other types of workers. This is all good news for people interested in entering the digital publishing field, which thrives on creativity.

So what is digital publishing and how does it impact our lives? To answer this, consider the ways in which we purchase a new car.

Without digital content at our fingertips, we might go to a library and read issues of *Consumer Reports* or the *Kelley Blue Book* to find out which car offers the features we are looking for at a price that works for our budget. Without digital information, we may find ourselves driving around town to visit the top five car dealerships to ask about pricing and warranty plans. We might end up calling a friend who owned a similar car to the one we're interested in to ask questions about maintenance and gas mileage. That's a lot of footwork for one purchase!

But because we have digital information at our fingertips, our car-purchasing experience is likely to be a lot easier and a lot quicker. At home on a laptop, we can access *Consumer Reports, Kelley Blue Book, Autotrader, NADAguides*, and a dozen other resources that can give us specs and testimonials

Making choices in today's burgeoning consumer marketplace is made easier thanks to digital publishing products such as online buyers' guides and consumer safety reports.

about the cars we're interested in. We can search online for pricing at all the dealerships in town.

When we arrive at the lot, we can use a phone to reference the car's VIN (vehicle identification number) history, which will tell us if it has been involved in any accidents or insurance claims. If we're still not sure, we can listen to car review podcasts or watch crash test videos on an iPad while having lunch. This sounds a lot more doable, doesn't it?

All these things and more are made possible through digital publishing. Online magazines, e-books, PDF catalogs, podcasts, and videos are all examples of digital content—the stuff that's at the heart of digital publishing. Distilled to a simple definition, digital publishing is the process of creating content that can be accessed by computer technology.

Jumping back to Adobe's report, survey respondents agreed that "technology and creativity go hand-in-hand." This makes the perfect tagline for the field of digital publishing. Publishing is about creation and design. And because our technology is constantly evolving, so, too, are opportunities in digital publishing.

Most notably, the independent book industry is booming, with women at the helm. Within traditional publishing, there is still a significant pay gap between men and women, partly because there are more men in managerial roles. However, indie publishing has provided many creative women with opportunities at all levels, from CEO to roles in editing and publicity. Meanwhile, initiatives such as the We Need Diverse Books campaign are creating more space for women and people of color in all areas of the publishing industry.

With all this in mind, there's never been a better time for young women to consider a career in digital publishing!

Chapter one

WHAT IS DIGITAL PUBLISHING?

D igital publishing, also referred to as online publishing or e-publishing, is an evolving field, intertwined with a variety of other industries. E-books, apps, infographics, and podcasts are all examples of digitally published content. Digital

Digital publishing allows us to access the content we want to read, watch, and listen to—from practically anywhere we want to be.

content is "anything that conveys ideas or information in a digital format." Content can be in the form of words, images, sound, or a combination of these.

THE "T" IN STEM

Science, technology, engineering, and mathematics are all fields that offer exciting and rewarding careers for women. Digital publishing falls in the category of technology because, at its core, it relies heavily upon computerized electronic devices.

Careers in digital publishing not only involve the production of digital content, but they also involve the dissemination of that content. Dissemination means "the sharing or circulation widely of something" and most often pertains to information or ideas. The ways we share information are crucial to successful communication—between friends or businesses— and the role technology plays in our communication is always evolving.

If you are interested in a career in digital publishing, there are three ways to get involved: design, creation, and dissemination.

DESIGN

Design refers to the phase when the technology used for digital publishing is imagined, constructed, and tested. Jobs in design include user-experience evaluation, software engineering, computer programming, and technical support.

CREATION

Creation refers to the phase when digital content is made using the technology built during the design phase. Jobs in creation include writing, editing, photography, graphic design, videography, audiography, and computer programming.

DISSEMINATION

Dissemination refers to the phase when the digital content made during the creation stage is published, organized, and marketed via electronic means. Jobs in dissemination include publishing, web development, digital asset management, and marketing.

Advances in both hardware and software and changing modes of communication require us to continually rethink the ways we engage colleagues and audiences. As innovators explore these new technologies, further opportunities in digital publishing will arise.

THE DIGITAL PUBLISHING REVOLUTION

In the mid- to late twentieth century, desktop publishing technology entered the playing field, making it easy for almost anyone to produce professional-looking documents and

(continued on the next page)

(continued from the previous page)

graphics. Desktop publishing refers to "the ability to design and create material for publication on a desktop or laptop computer."

Adobe Systems Incorporated was one of the pioneers of this technology, having created PostScript, one of the first programming languages to allow for simple and exact positioning of objects on a computer-generated screen. This was a big deal because, prior to PostScript, formatting documents for mass publication was no easy feat. It involved complicated lithography equipment and typesetting skills.

As desktop publishing became widely available, thanks to the growing use of personal computers, many people began to tinker with this new technology. No longer were professional-looking publications restricted to businesses and large organizations. Neighborhood groups and individuals now had the ability at their fingertips to create for print.

With the advent of the internet as a public forum for ideas and information sharing, desktop publishing as a skill set emerged as the basis for a whole new professional field. Chat rooms gave way to online journals, which then developed into blogs and online magazines. On a parallel trajectory, CD-ROM databases began to be accessed online and soon information was not only collected online, but also curated and created there. Digital publishing was born.

People were self-publishing in all manners online, from early social networks to self-published novels. The traditional book and magazine publishing companies were next to follow. Today, you can find almost any kind of content online.

THE DIGITAL PUBLISHING SKILL SET

Digital publishers work in a variety of industries. They collaborate with writers and editors as well as photographers and oral historians. They work alongside scientists, medical doctors, educators, and marketers. As technology continues to evolve, digital publishers are at the forefront of expanding the ways we communicate and share information.

Because of this, there are numerous opportunities to work within the field. There are also a wide variety of skills needed for success in the industry. Knowing how to review and edit digital media, understanding principles of design and layout, being able to analyze audience demographics and interests, knowing how to use digital publishing technology, keeping abreast of trends in communication, and understanding copyright and intellectual property laws—these are some of the many skills that professionals in digital publishing rely upon daily.

Although there are many different careers in digital publishing, successful professionals in the industry do have some things in common:

- Artistic ability: Whether or not they are working as creators, they should be able to evaluate creative digital work with an eye for visual appeal, legibility, and audience engagement.
- Strong communication skills: Collaboration is commonplace in publishing, so it is important to be able to effectively communicate ideas and get along with all sorts of people.

Creative collaborations are the backbone of the digital publishing industry. Agile communication and innovative thinking are present at every stage of the process.

- Attention to detail: To ensure a final product is accurate and appealing, digital-publishing professionals need to be able to spot potential problems at every stage of the process.
- Organizational skills: Digital publishing is a deadline-driven industry, so it's important to be able to manage your time efficiently and prioritize the most important tasks.

DIGITAL MEDIA QUEEN: TIFFANY PHAM

Listed as one of *Forbes*'s "30 Most Important Women Under 30" in media and technology, Tiffany Pham founded digital publishing platform and news aggregator Mogul. Pham created Mogul to help women worldwide raise their voices and connect with one another. The platform is visited by eighteen million users in more than 196 countries. Through partnerships with UN Women

TIFFANY PHAM

and similar organizations, Mogul invests a portion of company profits to help provide education to women in need around the globe.

Pham and Mogul have been nominated for and received a number of important distinctions, including Business Insider's "100 Most Exciting Startups of 2016" and *Entrepreneur* magazine's "Top Online Learning Platform." Additionally, she has served as a judge on the TLC show *Girl Starter* and continues to serve as a positive role model for women in the male-dominated Silicon Valley.

iffany Pham is a leader in digital publishing because she as pushed the medium to meet the changing needs of /omen worldwide.

INDUSTRY OPTIONS AND CHALLENGES

The sky is the limit when it comes to places to work in digital publishing. Because digital content comes in many forms—subscription, free distribution, open access, and paid circulation—and because it can be used to cover any topic—biology, engineering, social sciences, history, and literature—there are numerous places to look for work or internships.

In general, there are two ways to work as a professional in digital publishing. You can either work for an organization as a hired employee (with steady paychecks and benefits) or as a contracted freelancer (working on temporary projects for any number of organizations).

Organizations hiring professionals in the digital publishing field include traditional publishing houses or self-publishing houses, software firms, web consultancies, marketing firms, news organizations, database management companies, special or academic libraries, state or private archives, universities, or other organizations or individuals with a web presence.

Regardless of industry, digital publishers deal with many of the same issues and challenges: content distribution, mobile optimization, incorporation of analytics, monetization, and intellectual-property management, to name a few. Try to learn as much as you can about the industry of your interest so you can successfully navigate these challenges.

Chapter two

SOFTWARE DEVELOPERS

D esigning computer software is no easy feat. Much like building a skyscraper, the task of stacking code to build a multifunctional piece of software is a work of engineering. If a piece of code is faulty or incorrectly placed, the whole structure may collapse, just as a skyscraper would if built with the wrong type of materials.

If you want to get in on the behind-the-scenes action and help to design the technology behind digital publishing, perhaps a career as a software developer is right for you. Software development is a specialization within the discipline of computer science, which is the study of computers, their design, and their potential uses.

ON THE JOB

The software development process consists of several phases—each one with its own associated software development specialists. Applications software developers are the minds and imaginations behind the software built for the digital publishing field. Applications software developers work within systems that have already been built (for example, Windows or Mac operating systems).

These developers design software (such as word-processing or digital presentation programs) that will be compatible and function on different types of hardware. For example, an applications software developer assigned to work on the next version of Microsoft Word would need to make sure that the software functions well on desktops, laptops in tablet mode, and mobile devices like iPads and smartphones.

As a software developer, you may opt to play one of the following roles, or several, based on your experience and expertise:

USER-EXPERIENCE ENGINEER

The first thing engineers do before building a new piece of software is to evaluate similar software or previous versions of a software they are looking to update. Understanding how the software works to meet the goals of its users is crucial. This is called user experience, also referred to as UX. By studying how users expect to use and how they actually use a piece of software, software engineers learn how to proceed in the next stages of the software development process.

Among other things, user-experience engineers look at the following variables when evaluating software: overall ease of use, useful versus not useful features, accessibility for disabled users, and ease of navigation in finding software functions and content.

Designing a mobile app requires a strong sense of usability. Designers must understand how customers prefer to interact with a product's features.

User design for digital publishing may involve considering such things as word processing display options, font readability, typeface to HD display translation, and icon identification ease (for example, do users intuitively understand that a square with an arrow pointing down inside means "save"?).

SOFTWARE ENGINEER

After the goals of the user design have been determined, it's the job of a software engineer to develop system specifications alongside the design of the actual software. Software engineers are primarily concerned with developing algorithms, or sets of rules for the computer to follow to accomplish a task. Designing the software may be multifaceted, involving other software engineers with various levels of collaboration.

Software engineers in the digital publishing field may be concerned with how to build cross-platform readability (for example, when an app can be used in both iOS and Android), built-in analytics, and content packaging rules for selection by the user.

COMPUTER PROGRAMMER

When the software concept moves on to the next phase, it is ready to be written. Computer programmers are responsible for drafting and testing the code that will be pieced together to make the software function as it should for a reasonable period of time.

Because of the complexity of computer code, computer programmers have learned to package and reuse code. It is up to them to determine the best CASE (computer-assisted software engineering) tools to use to write the code that will be applied in building everything from successful digital publishing platforms to e-reader software for mobile devices.

TECHNICAL SUPPORT

Once a piece of software has been written, tested, and released, software developers continue to

Developing software for digital publishing may take a year or more, including various stages of design and testing over and over again.

provide support, even when the software is in the customer's hands. This means identifying and fixing bugs, providing software updates, and communicating with customer service specialists or the customers themselves in resolving problems. Technical support professionals address such concerns as continued optimization for mobile browsing, juggling advertising channels, and integrating social media.

GETTING INTO SOFTWARE DEVELOPMENT

The best way to know whether a career path is right for you is to spend some time learning what the job involves.

- If you're interested in software development, there are numerous free e-books and websites available online or through your local library or university. You may wish to take a look at the website Learn Code the Hard Way or check out the book *Structure and Interpretation of Computer Programs*.

- Learn about computer programming languages. Knowing how to talk to computers is key to understanding the premise of computer coding and software design. Spectrum, Python, Ruby, C, Java, and JavaScript were the top-used programming languages of 2017. Find out more at websites like CodeMentor or hackr.io.

- Teach yourself how to code. It has never been easier or more fun to learn this essential skill. There are numerous free apps and classes that can get you started. Try Girls Who Code, Alice, the MIT APP Inventor, Code Academy, or Khan Academy. Or find a local coding club through Hack Club or CoderDojo. Your local library may even offer coding workshops and clubs.

JOB OUTLOOK

At minimum, software developers in digital publishing typically have a bachelor's degree in computer science or mathematics and strong computer programming skills. When selecting coursework in college, look into classes related to building software, computer coding, and media and communications. Important qualities to develop include problem solving, analytical skills, and interpersonal communication.

Software development is a competitive field, requiring a lot of hard work and discipline. Learning how to work creatively on command is also a crucial skill.

Applications software developers working in digital publishing may work for publishing houses, software firms, news organizations, or social media enterprises. The typical work environment is an office setting where collaboration is encouraged. Telecommuters who work from home often use online project management spaces to collaborate with coworkers.

There are ample opportunities for advancement in the field and a number of paths to take. Software developers often move on to become IT systems managers, project leads, software engineering consultants, or even digital publishing platform designers.

The Bureau of Labor Statistics (BLS) projected a 17 percent growth in software development employment from 2014 to 2024. Job predictions within the subdisciplines of digital publishing software development are overwhelmingly positive, with nearly every related field showing a projected increase in job growth and creation. These fields include the information industry; software publishing; the motion picture, video, and sound recording industry; and the scientific and technical industry.

Chapter three

DIGITAL CONTENT CREATORS: WRITERS

Of course, there would be no field of digital publishing without the people who write the words and put together the concepts that fill our screens. These people are called content creators or writers. They create content that tells stories and shares facts and encourage participation with digital content through the creation of discussion forums, polls, and message boards.

DIGITAL CONTENT EXPLAINED

Digital content is anything that's made to be viewed on an electronic device. The most easily recognized types of content include websites and blogs, e-books, and mobile apps. But the list certainly doesn't end there.

Digital content can be textual, such as fictional stories, news articles, novellas and novels, memoirs and journals, employee handbooks, encyclopedia entries, résumés, and scientific papers. Digital content can also be audiovisual, such as videos, podcasts, vlogs, photo journals, clip art, brochures, and graphs and diagrams. Often, digital content is a

Writers produce content from fluff pieces to controversial articles. They write memes with cat photos as well as hard-hitting essays on culture and politics.

combination of textual and audiovisual components, such as marketing presentations, infographics, e-comics, portfolios, mobile apps, video games, and information databases.

Digital content arrives in many forms. You can subscribe to news sites and online journals and have them delivered to your email in-box. Or you can pay per item, like when you purchase an e-book on your phone or buy a game for your tablet. You can also access digital content by obtaining a membership to a streaming video or audio service. You don't own any of the videos or music you can access, but you have unlimited access to them on supported devices, such as your phone, computer, or even your game console. And because the internet is the biggest open access forum for information, there is a lot of digital content that can be accessed for free. Newsletters, podcasts, and even apps and e-books can be found for free on websites, online marketplaces, and social media.

GETTING INTO WRITING

Before you are hired as a writer, you will need to gain some practical experience. Experience will not only give you a better idea of your strengths and weaknesses, it will help you understand the best ways to improve, making you a stronger writer.

- Seek out an internship. Internships allow beginners to learn alongside working professionals. Many news agencies and magazines offer internships to help aspiring writers gain valuable on-the-job training.
- Join a creative writing group. Sharing your work with others will give you a broader perspective on the creative process. Additionally, you will strengthen your evaluation and editing skills through receiving and giving constructive feedback. Ask your local community center or public library or find a group online. Some online communities worth checking out

(continued on the next page)

(continued from the previous page)

include Absolute Write Water Cooler, Mibba, National Novel Writing Month, WritersCafe, and the Reddit Writer's Group.
- Find a mentor in the business. A mentor can help you connect with solid resources for learning, practicing, and meeting other professionals in the field. You could try finding a mentor through a school guidance counseling program or via one of these organizations: MentorNet, GirlVentures, CyberMentor, and Young Women Rock! of the Women Worldwide Initiative.

WRITERS ON THE JOB

Although digital content is becoming increasingly multimedia, textual content continues to serve as the backbone of the digital publishing industry. After all, even photographs are best experienced with the aid of a caption.

Often, a writer's work is needed during the development stages of multimedia content. For example, films and podcasts sometimes rely upon written scripts, show notes, and stage directions, which are prepared by a writer prior to recording or publication. Writers are also responsible for the content found in advertisements, magazines, books, songs, blogs, reports, and more.

Writers may work for any number of organizations or businesses, including news agencies, publishing

After an actor reads through a script, rewriting is often required. Digital writers need to be able to hear and apply constructive feedback.

houses, content mills, and websites, depending on the type of work they perform:

- Copywriters prepare material, called copy, for advertisements. Copy is written in a specific style based on marketing briefs, which are guidelines to help the writer match content with specific audiences. They work with clients or through agencies to promote the sale of goods or services.

- Journalists write reports, articles, and news items related to current events. They typically work with news agencies and magazines.
- Bloggers write online content related to specific topics or fields of interest, such as lifestyle, pets, entrepreneurship, and technology. Bloggers often work with a variety of clients, including businesses and individuals.
- Creative writers work in a plethora of mediums. Some write novels and plays, while others write screenplays or songs. They sell their work to publishing houses, media producers, or even private organizations.

Most writers use computers to compose their work. They either work from home or out of an office. Although writing is primarily a desk job, writers will often perform on-the-ground research to obtain factual information and authentic detail. Writing for publication typically involves several work phases, from taking notes and conducting interviews, to drafting and editing.

JOB OUTLOOK

Although not required in many cases, a college degree is often preferred for content creators working in salaried positions as writers. Writers typically study English literature, composition, creative writing, journalism, or communications.

Of course, writers need to be creative and good at writing. Other skills that are important for

WHAT IS A GHOSTWRITER?

A ghostwriter is a writer hired to write content that will be credited to another person. A ghostwriter is typically contracted to work on a specific project and must sign an NDA, or nondisclosure agreement. This agreement is sometimes part of a contract wherein the writer agrees to meet specific goals while remaining quiet about his or her authorship role.

Often, someone will hire a ghostwriter when that person has a story to tell but not necessarily the writing skills to craft his or her own story. Many celebrities, politicians, and executives rely upon ghostwriters. Even bestselling authors, such as Tom Clancy, have been known to use ghostwriters to produce commercial fiction at a quick pace.

successful writers include attention to detail, critical thinking, social perceptiveness, persuasiveness, determination, and a knowledge of trends in their field of interest.

According to the Bureau of Labor Statistics, job growth for writers was expected to grow roughly 2 percent from 2014 to 2024. While this is a little slower than some occupations within the field of digital publishing, many content creators don't exclusively focus on a single type of creative work. A lot of digital content creators produce crossover work, combining textual with audiovisual work.

Although a certain amount of talent is certainly involved, writers become good at their work through practice. There is always more to learn.

Advancement for writers often includes opportunities in editing and publishing or lateral moves, such as working in design or publicity. Writers should stay on top of technological developments that affect the field of digital publishing. It is also a good idea to obtain some business knowledge, such as understanding how to manage your finances, file taxes, promote your business, organize clients, and manage projects. These skills will enable you to grow as a professional while making you a valuable freelancer or employee.

Chapter four

VISUAL CONTENT CREATORS: GRAPHIC DESIGNERS AND PHOTOGRAPHERS

t is often said that a picture is worth a thousand words. While words tell us names and facts, images can convey mood and emotions—things that can be more difficult to show through text. And while written words are indeed an important part of the digital publishing industry, visual elements make digital content stand out. If you're interested in creating visual content for the digital realm, you may want to consider a career in graphic design, photography, or another kind of visual art.

GRAPHIC DESIGNERS ON THE JOB

Graphic designers are the creators behind the visual concepts found in digital content—icons, logos, illustrations, typefaces, and stylized data in the form of graphs, charts, and infographics. They are often responsible for designing the layout and overall style of the digital publication. They may work at design

Developing your own sense of style is important, but freelance graphic designers also need to be able to adjust to the styles of the organizations they work for.

firms, advertising or public relations companies, publishing houses, or printing companies.

The graphic designer begins by meeting with the client or art director. They discuss the project's goals and the particular style needed to achieve those goals. Depending on the scope of the project, there may be several feedback phases built into the timeline. Before turning in the final work, the designer will present ideas, incorporate feedback, and review for errors.

WHAT IS AN INFOGRAPHIC?

Infographics are multimedia platforms used to share information. They can best be described as digital posters. In business and media, they are used to convey information, often in conjunction with a report, as a way to make that information more engaging and easily digestible.

Infographics are usually created as a graphics file, which can be pasted or embedded into another type of file—for instance, on a website or within a document. An infographic uses diagrams, icons, statistics, keywords, and text to convey information in an intuitive and visual manner. It is often created with design principles in mind, using interesting fonts, engaging information flow, and pleasing color palettes.

According to the Bureau of Labor Statistics, one in five graphic designers was self-employed in 2014. Most graphic designers work full time, although some perform graphic design work in addition to other roles at a creative firm. They typically work in offices or studios where they have access to art supplies, drafting equipment, and design software. And they use a combination of digital and hands-on tools to communicate concepts that are relevant to the publication.

Graphic designers need to make sure their work is relevant to an audience that is always evolving. Other challenges include working with technology that is regularly updated and scaling layout, which means making sure the content is readable and the style is consistent no matter the reading device—website, mobile app, wearable tech, or e-reader.

Graphic designers may have the opportunity to advance to positions of greater responsibility as project leads, chief designers, or art directors.

PHOTOGRAPHERS ON THE JOB

Photographers use cameras and camera equipment to compose, frame, record, and edit photographic imagery. They use various photographic techniques, lenses, and lighting equipment to capture scenes and subjects in high-quality digital files.

The photographs are used in digital content to express ideas, tell stories, and convey emotions. Stock shots are photographs taken of products, categories of things, people performing actions, and signs that have commercial applications in advertising and graphic design.

There are various types of specialties that a photographer can choose to pursue:

- Portrait photographers photograph individuals or groups of people. They work in their own studios or on location and are hired by individuals and organizations to record special moments and events. Portrait photographers in the digital publishing industry are often hired to take professional headshots.

- Commercial and industrial photographers work with images of products, services, facilities, models, and landscapes. They can be freelance or salaried and work on-site or within corporate or rented studios. As digital content becomes more widely used, many freelance photographers have success selling their work to stock photography sites such as Dreamstime or Stock Photography.
- Aerial photographers, who previously might have relied on helicopters and planes, now use

During a product photo session, a digital photographer may take over a thousand photos, using different props, lighting, and even sets.

drones to capture photographs of building sites, landscapes, pipelines, and remote industrial operations. These photographs can be used for land-use analysis, real estate, and industry websites and reports.

GETTING INTO DIGITAL VISUAL ARTS

If you're interested in creating visual art for digital publishing, it's highly likely that you are already experimenting with art and art techniques. That is great! There are a number of other ways you can prepare for a successful career in digital visual arts:

- Take a class. Begin by seeking out classes at your school or recreation center. Local universities often offer summer courses for all ages. Ask your library for educational resources like Lynda.com or Gale Courses or try out a massive open online course (MOOC) through Coursera or edX.
- Read about your interests. Visit the websites of artists, graphic designers, and photographers to read about other people's journeys in the realm of visual art.
- View online tutorials. Due to the visual nature of the work, it can be helpful to watch design tutorials to give yourself an idea of the kind of work that is possible with various computerized tools. Tutorials can be found on product websites (such as Adobe Creative Cloud), creative communities (like DigitalArts or CreativeBloq), and of course, YouTube.

JOB OUTLOOK

If you are looking to work with a firm or company, you are likely to need a bachelor's degree in art, graphic design, or a similar discipline. For freelance work, a degree can be useful, but it is often not required. In fact, much of the work of a graphic designer, photographer, or other visual artist can be learned on the job.

You may be interested in taking classes in studio art, principles of design, commercial graphics

Graphic design for digital publishing may require an understanding of real-world objects and tools, like those found in augmented-reality publications and games.

production, software design suites, digital media, or publishing. These courses are available both online and in person at universities, private art collectives, and continuing education or certificate programs.

To work in visual arts for the digital publishing industry, you need to be tech savvy and willing to continue to learn to use new platforms and software. Also, because visual artists are often juggling multiple projects, time management and organizational skills are crucial.

Because of the continuing shift toward digital content in the publishing industry, there will be an increasing need for graphic designers as organizations and businesses seek visually appealing and user-friendly media. According to the Bureau of Labor Statistics, job opportunities for graphic designers working in the computer industry were projected to increase by 21 percent from 2014 to 2024. Opportunities for photographers were projected to see a smaller yet still significant increase of 9 percent over the same period of time.

Chapter five

EDITORS, PUBLISHERS, AND WEB DEVELOPERS

O f the many careers available in the digital publishing industry, editors and publishers are perhaps the best known. They work closely with content creators to refine content and target ideal audiences for the content they publish. Web developers perform similar roles in regard to the design and launch of websites.

Often, the roles of editors and publishers are intertwined, and in smaller presses, the editor may also be the publisher. For those interested in working in digital publishing, it's important to understand the distinctions.

EDITORS ON THE JOB

Editors plan, review, and revise content for publication. In each of these phases, there are numerous considerations, depending on the breadth of the editor's role. An important part of the planning phase is content curation, which means seeking out and selecting the content. The content an editor seeks will be defined by the mission and audience of the publication. Editors are responsible for developing upcoming themes, selecting promising proposals for further consideration, contracting writers and designers, and implementing timelines.

Editors usually review content during the writing process. When editors review content, they are generally checking to make sure the content matches the publishing house's style, language levels, and formatting specifications for digital publication. A review of content in progress can also help an author hone in on what's missing or not working in her writing.

The editing phase most often occurs after a completed manuscript or draft of the content is turned in by the creator. Editing can be performed on several levels, including developmental editing, line editing, and copyediting. This means that editors will review and edit the content based on larger concepts, like theme and structure, as well as on smaller things, like grammar and punctuation. Audiovisual editing is another consideration for the digital publishing editor. This can entail visual formatting and layout considerations such as readability or audio quality, content flow, visual appeal, and user experience.

Editors typically juggle multiple projects at the same time and, as such, often employ the help of slush readers and editorial assistants. Editing content can result in multiple drafts until the final product meets the approval of publisher, editor, and creator. Because of the diverse nature of digital content, editors need to be comfortable using and learning new digital technologies. Whether they work from

Editors, publishers, and web developers must think strategically. They should understand how their content will connect with and engage their readers.

home or from an office, editors in digital publishing must be knowledgeable about digital communication tools, such as social media, and digital rights management software.

PUBLISHERS ON THE JOB

Publishers, much like CEOs, provide structure and guidelines for the general business of the publishing house. They will often be involved in stakeholder discussions and reporting, industry collaboration and networking, and other high-level operations.

Publishers have oversight of the entire process. They are responsible for determining the direction of the publication. This includes setting the mission and selecting the prime audiences to target for content and advertising. Publishers also work closely with the financial team to set sales goals and allocate funds for the various departments of the publishing house. To meet goals and make profitable sales, they craft business strategy plans that outline the overall tone of the publishing house.

Publishers are also responsible for the distribution avenues of their content—whether their material is available at stores or in various e-formats—and they must stay on top of trends in digital publishing, including search engine optimization (SEO) and publishing technologies. Along with these responsibilities, they must be well versed in copyright law.

Successful publishers are knowledgeable about the publishing industry, understanding the strengths and weaknesses of the digital format and how best to reach their audience within that format. They also have a thorough understanding of each phase and each role within the industry. Many publishers began by gaining experience in other capacities within the field, such as working as editors, publicists, or even content creators.

GETTING INTO EDITING AND PUBLISHING

To be an editor, you will need to know the basics of composition and grammar. To be a publisher, it's important to understand the industry. Here are some ideas for preparing yourself for these professions:

- **Make sure you understand composition and grammar rules and applications.** There are a lot of fun and interesting grammar books that make learning these things easy and entertaining. Look for *The Deluxe Transitive Vampire,* by Karen Elizabeth Gordon, *Eats, Shoots & Leaves,* by Lynne Truss, or *Sin and Syntax,* by Constance Hale.

- **Understand the business.** Two highly regarded online publications devoted to the industry are Publishers Weekly and Publishing Perspectives. Visit these regularly to learn the ins and outs of how publishing works.

- **Learn how to communicate professionally.** Providing valuable feedback to content creators is an important skill. This often means learning how to work with different personalities and navigating interpersonal communication. You can work on your people skills by joining a club, volunteering with a service-based organization, or viewing online tutorials on interpersonal skills.

- **Consider working on your school newspaper or yearbook**. This is often a good place to start as you learn how to work as a team to produce a final published product.

WEB DEVELOPERS

Web developers design and create websites, and websites are, of course, one of the most widely used platforms for digital content. Emerging technologies and apps make it quick and easy for people to create their own websites, but for those wishing to make a career out of website development, there's a lot more to learn.

Web developers are hired by organizations, companies, and individuals to create, maintain, and update websites. They are responsible for the overall look and feel of the site, including technical aspects such as user experience, performance speed, and traffic capacity. For smaller organizations, web developers often find themselves playing multiple roles, including editor, graphic designer, and content creator.

Web developers fall into three categories:

- Back-end developers build the structure behind the scenes of a website. They create the forms and framework that can be used to display and share content. They are responsible for designing the site's style and overseeing the creative development.
- Front-end developers use the frameworks built by the back-end developers to create a specific page that the user engages with. They control content layout and integrate graphics,

Successful web development is a collaborative process involving writers, designers, editors, permissions experts, software designers, clients, and others.

audiovisual content, widgets, and integrated applications.

- Webmasters are the day-to-day maintainers of websites. They roll out changes, respond to complaints on the site's use, fix bugs, and communicate analytics, or website use information, with the site's owner.

GETTING INTO WEB DEVELOPMENT

Web developers should hone their skills to make them stand out as professionals. It's easy to begin learning how to navigate the web and how to create webpages. You can begin by creating your own website using an existing platform such as WordPress or Weebly.

Try these activities to expand your knowledge of web development basics:

- Learn HTML and experiment with altering components of your site using this programming language. HTML is a computer language that is easy to use. It can help you alter such things as font size, style, and color. Paired with more complex lines of code, you can use HTML to change up your spacing and layout to make your site easy to read and intuitive to use.
- Install some widgets that appeal to your audience and encourage engagement. Widgets, such as counters, slideshows, or add-in forums, can enhance your site by making it more user friendly or interactive. Often, adding widgets and making them fit where you want them requires some fiddling with HTML. See what's available for your chosen platform and have fun making it unique.
- Research your demographic. Who reads your site and how can you grow your audience? Explore various ways to learn about your audience through use and analysis of analytics programs such as Google Analytics.

JOB PREPARATION

Editors and publishers often have degrees in English language or composition, communications, or journalism. They may also study business, marketing, or management. Both editors and publishers must be detail oriented and have strong writing skills, good judgment, and top-notch interpersonal skills.

Web developers often have degrees in computer science or programming. At minimum, an associate's degree in web design can provide the basic building blocks for working in web development. It also helps to have a solid knowledge of computer programming and graphic design.

JOB OUTLOOK

As the publishing industry continues to shift from print to digital content, editors and publishers who have adapted to the digital publishing realm will have a distinct advantage over those who are trained only in traditional publishing. Moreover, according to a 2017 study by SembraMedia, the digital publishing industry is creating record numbers of positions for women at the top levels.

Editors, publishers, and web developers in the evolving digital publishing industry should be prepared to take on multiple roles. They will need to understand digital rights management and learn about marketing techniques for evolving audiences, as well as being nimble enough to navigate the changing face of the publishing industry.

Chapter six

GETTING THE JOB

When preparing for your job hunt, there are several crucial steps to making sure you are a top candidate for your perfect job. Among those steps, you'll want to know how to build a rock-solid résumé, craft an enticing cover letter, and prepare yourself for a successful interview. If you're diligent and thoughtful, preparing for the job search can be a valuable experience in and of itself.

BUILDING YOUR RÉSUMÉ

Your résumé is an important part of the job application process. It paints a picture of you that search committees and hiring managers will see before they meet you face to face. In most cases, your résumé determines whether potential employees want to meet you at all. Because of this, you want to make sure it does an excellent job representing you and your skills.

A strong résumé speaks directly to those hiring. It is easy to read and concise. While you'll want to begin work on your résumé before the job search, you'll need to remember to revisit it once you've found a specific job listing that interests you.

CONTENT

At minimum, your résumé should reveal your education, your professional experience, and any valuable skills that you could rely upon or contribute as a potential employee. It should also include your full name and contact info in a prominent location.

When it comes to your education, most employers want to know the type and discipline of your degree and when you obtained it. It can also be helpful to include a strong GPA or any involvement in an honors program. Unless you have no professional experience, your education section should be a simple listing—no detailed description needed.

Your professional experience is usually the most relevant part for potential employers. They will want to know where you've worked, for how long, what your title was, and what your job entailed. It can also be helpful to include work you did on special projects, especially those where you held a leadership position.

Use power verbs to describe the work you performed. Power verbs are concise and accurate. They help to paint an active picture of what you did. For example, use "facilitated" instead of "led" to describe a task involving giving guided tours with a hands-on component. "Led," while an everyday term, is too simple and merely implies that you took a tour group from point A to point B. "Facilitated" is more precise as it implies both leadership of a group and guidance through some sort of interactive component. Other power verbs you could use to describe a leadership role might include: changed, conducted, directed, empowered, enlisted, guided, initiated, mentored, spearheaded, and transformed.

A skills section is another key feature of your résumé. For jobs in digital publishing, hiring managers always like to know if you are already proficient in design and editing software. Other hot skill sets include languages, grant application work, and leadership skills.

Of course, you don't need to stop there. Other features that you may wish to add include:

- An objective statement—stating what you're looking for and why you're the ideal match (ideally one sentence).
- Volunteer experience—remember to align the experiences you list with the job for which you are applying.
- A creative portfolio—this applies to jobs with a visual or creative aspect; create an online portfolio and provide the link.

When you revisit your résumé after finding a job you are interested in applying for, you'll want to link keywords. Look closely at the terms used in the job description to describe requirements and responsibilities. Ask yourself if any of those terms could be used to describe your experience and be sure to use those terms in your résumé.

STYLE

It used to be the case that style was not important in résumés. However, in the era of digital content,

When designing your résumé, consider which information should be shown chronologically and which should be shown from a functional perspective.

we are shifting toward a more visual culture. Visually appealing résumés are now accepted and may even be preferred if you are applying to jobs with a visual component.

Style cannot interfere with readability, though. Bold or large type should be used sparingly to denote headings, titles, and dates. Fonts should be easy to read. Avoid the fancier fonts with lots of curlicues or graphical embellishments. If you're not sure whether to use a font, take a look at something written in that font from a distance to see if you can still read it.

When you are adding graphical elements, think about the job for which you are applying. Elements such as icons, photographs, illustrations, and mini infographics can certainly make your résumé stand out, but you'll want to use discretion when deciding how to apply them. For jobs in graphic design, your résumé could serve as a view into your style. But if you're applying for a writing job, graphical elements may be seen as a way to avoid using language.

LOOKING FOR A JOB

When looking for work in the digital publishing field, there are a few ways to go about it. The most important thing you can do is educate yourself about the industry—the companies involved, the movers and shakers, and the technology. Once you have some background knowledge to work with, take a look at company websites, LinkedIn profiles, Facebook groups devoted to specific types of work, job-hunting sites, and professional organizations.

Some good general ones to look into include the Association of American Publishers (specifically the Committee for Digital Information), the Graphic Artists Guild, the Software Publishers Association, the International Digital Publishing forum, the Editorial Freelancers' Association, and the American Copy Editors' Society. Keep in mind that there are even more niche organizations, depending upon your specific interests.

Most of these professional organizations offer membership levels for students and special

Not only will professional connections help you practice your elevator pitch, but they often also lead to lasting professional relationships and future opportunities.

discounted prices for conference attendance. Attending a professional conference can be a truly valuable experience. Not only will you be able to sit in on workshops and presentations about various innovations and challenges in the field, but you will also have the opportunity to network.

When you find a job that interests you, read the description carefully. Look for keywords that match your experience. Pay attention to applicant requirements, preferred qualities, and expectations. Make sure you understand the position, and do a little research if you have any questions.

THE MAGIC COVER LETTER

After your résumé, your cover letter is the most important thing that potential employers will see. Don't skimp on the work on this application step! Take the time to write a friendly and compelling letter.

Here are some rock-solid tips to strengthen your letter:

- Limit your letter to one page.
- Use a professional but friendly tone. Confident but respectful enthusiasm will always stand out.
- Highlight a few of your experiences that align with the candidate profile they are seeking.
- Demonstrate knowledge of the field and the kind of work you'd be performing in this role.
- Describe your skills with action verbs and active voice.
- Thank them for taking the time to review your application.

Each cover letter you write should be unique. You are applying for a specific opportunity, so you should tailor the letter to that job. Finally, before you submit your application materials, don't forget to review everything for content, punctuation, spelling (especially of names), and verb tenses.

ACING YOUR INTERVIEW

When you've been invited to interview, the first thing you should do is thank the interviewer for the opportunity. Once you've got a date and time

An interview is your opportunity to show potential employers what you would contribute to the workplace. It also demonstrates how well you think on your feet.

set up, it's time to do your homework. Do some research into the company. Take a look at the mission statement, recent news, and ongoing projects. Make sure you understand the role you would be playing and consider possible challenges and how you might handle them. Practice your answers to both informative questions (What did you do at Company Press?) and behavioral questions (How would you respond to critical feedback from a colleague?) you might be asked in the interview.

On the day of your interview, arrive a few minutes early. Dress professionally and bring a few extra copies of your résumé. Make sure you've prepared a few targeted questions in advance and bring these with you. It never hurts to bring along a notebook and a pen; it can help to jot notes down as your interviewers ask multipart questions or give you important information to consider about the job. When answering questions, remember to use eye contact and positive body language. Don't be afraid to ask the interviewers to repeat or clarify questions.

Write down all the names of the individuals on the hiring team. After the interview, don't forget to send individual thank-you notes. A quick and personalized thank-you email shows that you value that person's time and appreciate the opportunity to interview.

Chapter seven

THE DIGITAL PUBLISHING PROFESSIONAL

What does it mean to be a professional? Do your actions, behavior, habits, and communication style really matter? The answer is an unequivocal yes! Being a professional means more than just doing the job. It means performing and producing work with integrity.

Once you have a job in digital publishing, it's time to work on being as professional as possible. This is how you turn a job into a long and rewarding career.

HOW TO BE A PROFESSIONAL

When you are a professional, your coworkers have faith in your comportment and your communications, as well as your technical abilities. They trust that you will do your job well and that when there are bumps in the road, you will assess and tackle them in a timely and efficient manner.

Technical skills are a part of being successful in a digital publishing career, but beyond being able to perform the day-to-day work, there are a number of soft skills that are crucial to being seen as a professional.

SELF-IMPROVEMENT

Seek out opportunities to participate in continuing education opportunities such as professional reading, workshop participation, conference attendance, and personal development programs. You can do this by joining a professional organization, such as the Association of American Publishers, or enrolling in a certificate program like the Summer Publishing Institute through New York University's School of Professional Studies. Those short on time and resources can keep up with trends in the field by subscribing to professional networks, trend reports, and technology trials. The websites of *Publishers Weekly*, Publishing Trends, What's New in Publishing, and State of Digital Publishing are all useful places to look.

However, professional development shouldn't interfere with the job itself or with your personal life. Maintaining a healthy work-life balance is another important skill to master. Many successful professionals struggle in this area, so keep it on your radar and start strong by setting boundaries and learning about time management.

INTERPERSONAL SKILLS

Professionals in all areas of digital publishing need to be able to communicate ideas, resolve conflicts, and

Networking is useful for learning about industry trends, bouncing ideas off other professionals, and learning about new opportunities for growth and improvement.

encourage innovation. Having strong interpersonal skills can help you to motivate and direct employees, which in turn can lead to leadership opportunities. After all, knowing how to coach a team through the creative process is pretty much daily work for a digital publishing leader.

The best way to improve your interpersonal skills is to read about the topic and reflect on your own strengths and weaknesses. Many people who have weak communication skills may not even realize that they need improvement. Think about whether you need to work on your verbal, nonverbal, and listening skills. Beyond those, you can branch out into learning about bigger, more complex skills, including emotional intelligence, negotiation, conflict resolution, and problem solving. In the digital publishing industry, you will be working with people with diverse skill sets and communication skills. Being able to master complicated tasks such as team building and conflict resolution within a group will make you a boon to any organization.

COMPORTMENT

It's not the shoes you choose to wear but how you wear them, right? It's actually a little of both. Comportment refers to both a professional appearance and a professional bearing. This means that professionals not only appear well groomed, but they also comport themselves in a respectful and confident manner. A professional comportment also refers to the ability to build trust and confidence in yourself. This means that you arrive on time, you are prepared, and you contribute.

Of course, there are many other ways to work on your professionalism, aside from self-improvement, interpersonal skills, and comportment. There's creative thinking, assertiveness, change management, and presentation skills. Take some time to read about professionals in your field to find out more.

For professionals in the digital publishing industry, building a positive reputation at work is key to job mobility and a happy work life.

SUCCESSFUL WOMEN IN DIGITAL PUBLISHING

It takes a combination of passion, skill, and professionalism to become a leader in your field. These successful women show us that the sky is the limit when it comes to reaching your potential as a tech girl in digital publishing:

JUANITA LEÓN, POLITICAL REPORTER

Cofounder and publisher of the award-winning digital news journal *La Silla Vacía* Juanita León and her team have produced timely, relevant reporting on Colombian politics and the South American political landscape. León won the Garcia Márquez journalism award for her coverage of the peace talks in Colombia. She has also been applauded for the data visualization published by her team on *La Silla Vacía,* featuring profiles of the powerful players in the Colombian government.

SOCIAL JUSTICE PUBLISHER SILKE K. BADER

Bader is the publisher of a handful of magazines that amplify the voices of the LGBTQ community in Australia, the United States, and western Europe. Driven by a desire to create change and work for social justice for people of all genders and sexualities, Bader successfully launched Australia's first lesbian magazine, *LOTL,* in both print and digital format, as one of the digital publishing platform Realview's first clients. She is also the publisher of *Curve* magazine in the United States and *DIVA*, Europe's bestselling lesbian magazine. Although she is a successful and accomplished businesswoman, she still makes a point to sit on community boards in an effort to continue learning about her community and audience.

YOUR FIRST WEEK ON THE JOB

Your first week at a new job can be exciting and overwhelming. Here are some tips and tricks to help you survive your first week while setting yourself up for long-term success:

- Take notes. Bring a notebook and pen everywhere. Write down names and titles and jot notes on who does what and key terms that your supervisor shares when discussing your responsibilities.
- Ask questions. In your first week, you have a lot of leeway—you won't be expected to know everything right off the bat. Ask questions about assignments as well as business norms for your organization. But avoid gossip whenever you can.
- Thank those who help. You'll be introduced to a lot of new information and a lot of new names. Be sure to thank those who spend time helping you get to know the ropes. A note or email can go a long way to helping you connect.

HOLY, EDITOR OF UNTOUCHD MAGAZINE

Described as the *Vogue* of tech, *UNTOUCHD* launched in 2015. Holy, the editor behind *UNTOUCHD*, says she was inspired by her little sister to create a magazine that would inspire other tech girls. Holy shares her love of coding and technology through her social media accounts and through the

Not only is Lyndsey Scott passionate about her work, but she is also passionate about mentoring other young women and helping them to realize their dreams.

mission of her magazine. She also contributes to her community through her involvement with the Atlanta chapter of Girl Develop It, a nonprofit organization that provides affordable programs for adult women to learn web and software development.

MODEL PROGRAMMER LYNDSEY SCOTT

Computer programmer Lyndsey Scott is also an actress and supermodel. She graduated from Amherst College with a double major in computer science and theater and has been working in both fields since. She has developed several creative apps, including imDown, a collaborative video community, beautifulBook, a design and font application, a couple of photography apps, and Educate!, an app devoted to helping young leaders in Africa. Most recently, Scott created RYSE UP, a talent and creative connection app.

It's easy to see that the field of digital publishing is diverse, exciting, and still evolving. Accomplished women from all walks of life have found the digital realm to be an open and welcome platform for a variety of creative publishing projects. In the years ahead, digital publishing will continue to provide opportunities for tech girls interested in creating, collaborating, and sharing with the world.

Glossary

AGGREGATOR Software, app, or website that collects and compiles a specific type of information.

ANALYTICS A process of discovering and analyzing data to identify patterns and determine useful applications of data.

AUDIOGRAPHY Recording and producing audio or sound recordings.

BLOG A simple platform for digital publishing, commonly in the form of a journal with separate posts or pages appearing in chronological order.

CONTENT MILL A sometimes derogatory term used to describe a company or organization that provides content that is designed only to appear in searches, generating page views that will result in advertising revenue.

CROSS-PLATFORM READABILITY The ease with which a piece of content can be viewed or read on multiple electronic devices.

DESKTOP PUBLISHING A broad set of skills required in the design and publication of materials using personal computers.

DIGITAL ASSET MANAGEMENT (DAM) The management of digital data, including selection, annotation, cataloging, storage, and retrieval of data.

DIGITAL CONTENT Textual, graphic, or audio information stored in digital data, also referred to as digital media.

DIGITAL PUBLISHING The electronic publication of digital content, also referred to as online publishing or e-publishing.

DIGITAL RIGHTS MANAGEMENT (DRM) Technologies developed to control access to copyrighted works and proprietary software.

DISSEMINATE To spread or circulate something widely, typically used in reference to information.

INDEPENDENT PUBLISHER A publishing house not affiliated with a large corporation or conglomerate.

INTELLECTUAL PROPERTY A work or invention, such as a manuscript or a design, to which the creator has rights.

MONETIZATION The act of making money from a product or service.

OPEN ACCESS A term used to refer to software that is free of license restrictions, wherein the code can be altered to suit a specific purpose.

SCALABILITY Term used to describe the ability of a website or online application to function with an increasing number of users.

SEARCH ENGINE OPTIMIZATION (SEO) The process of routing traffic to a site through the use of keywords, understanding search algorithms, and content architecture.

SLUSH READER A first reader who works with editors in weeding out weak submissions from unsolicited manuscripts, often called the slush pile.

STOCK PHOTOGRAPHY Photos of common places, things, events, or people that are bought and sold on a royalty-free basis and can be used for commercial purposes.

USER EXPERIENCE (UX) The overall experience of a person using a product, such as a digital program or application, and the degree to which it is easy or pleasing to use.

VIDEOGRAPHY Filming, editing, and producing video.

For More Information

Association of American Publishers
455 Massachusetts Avenue NW, Suite 700
Washington, DC 20001
(202) 347-3375
Website: http://publishers.org
Facebook: @AmericanPublishers
Twitter: @AmericanPublish
An American organization devoted to the
    publishing industry, providing professional
    networking, education, trend analysis, and
    updates to members.

Book and Periodical Council
174 Spadina Avenue, Suite 107
Toronto, ON M5T 2C2
Canada
(416) 975-9366
Website: http://www.thebpc.ca
A governmental and professional organization
    devoted to the publishing industry in Canada.
    It provides educational resources and
    opportunities for those working in the field,
    as well as keeping members informed about
    updates to the industry and technology.

BookNet Canada
401 Richmond Street West, Suite 376
Toronto, Ontario, M5V 1X3
Canada
Website: https://www.booknetcanada.ca

Facebook: @BookNetCanada
Twitter: @BookNet_Canada
BookNet Canada is a network for publishing
  professionals. It offers an annual leading industry
  event with platforms for discussing technology,
  the digital divide, inclusion, and accessibility in
  the publishing world.

Digital Media Association
1050 17th Street NW, Suite 520
Washington, DC 20036
(202) 639-9509
Website: http://www.digmedia.org
This national trade organization focuses
  on promoting business and regulatory
  environments that support its members in the
  digital media industry.

Free Software Foundation
51 Franklin Street, 5th Floor
Boston, MA 02110
(617) 542-5942
Website: http://www.fsf.org
Twitter: @fsf
A foundation created to promote "computer user
  freedom," the Free Software Foundation has a
  number of international chapters. They promote
  computing resources, most notably free or open-
  source software.

Girls Who Code
Website: https://girlswhocode.com
Facebook, Twitter, and Instagram: @GirlsWhoCode
A nonprofit organization devoted to helping girls
    succeed in STEM-related studies and careers.
    It offers nationwide programs on computer
    programming and coding.

International Digital Publishing Forum (IDPF)
113 Cherry Street, Suite 70-719
Seattle, WA 98104
(206) 451-7250
Website: http://idpf.org
The IDPF provides a forum for discussions on
    issues of interest and concern within the digital
    publishing field. It is known for developing
    industry standards such as file formats.

International Journalist's Network (IJNET)
2000 M Street NW, Suite 250
Washington, DC 20036
(202) 737-3700
Website: https://ijnet.org/en
Facebook and Twitter: @IJNet
IJNET disseminates the latest information on global
    media networks, innovation, new apps and tools,
    professional training, and jobs in journalism.

For Further Reading

Anton, Kelly Kordes. *Adobe InDesign CC Classroom in a Book.* New York, NY: Adobe Press, 2016.

Benke, Karen. *Leap Write In! Adventures in Creative Writing to Stretch and Surprise Your One-of-a-Kind Mind.* Boston, MA: Roost Books, 2013.

Bierut, Michael. *How to Use Graphic Design to Sell Things, Explain Things, Make Things Look Better, Make People Laugh, Make People Cry, and (Every Once in a While) Change the World.* New York, NY: Harper Design, 2015.

Browne, Renni. *Self-Editing for Fiction Writers: How to Edit Yourself into Print.* New York, NY: William Morrow Paperbacks, 2004.

Gordon, Karen Elizabeth. *The Deluxe Transitive Vampire: The Ultimate Handbook of Grammar for the Innocent, the Eager, and the Doomed.* New York, NY: Pantheon, 1993.

Harmon, Daniel. *Powering Up a Career in Software Development and Programming.* New York, NY: Rosen Publishing, 2016.

Kidd, Chip. *Go: A Kidd's Guide to Graphic Design.* New York, NY: Workman Publishing, 2014.

Pelos, Rebecca. *Cool Careers Without College for People Who Love Writing and Blogging.* New York, NY: Rosen Publishing, 2018.

Rogers, Scott. *Level Up! The Guide to Great Video Game Design.* New York, NY: Wiley, 2014.

Schmermund, Elizabeth. *Women in Technology* (Defying Convention: Women Who Changed the Rules). New York, NY: Enslow Publishing, 2017.

Bibliography

Adobe Systems Incorporated. "State of Create: 2016." November 1, 2016. http://www.adobe .com/content/dam/acom/en/max/pdfs /AdobeStateofCreate_2016_Report_Final.pdf.

Boyer, Justin. "History of Women in Software Engineering." Simple Programmer, September 18, 2017. https://simpleprogrammer .com/2017/09/18/female-software-engineers.

Breiner, James. "Women Take the Lead in Latin America's Digital Media Startup Landscape." International Journalists' Network, August 16, 2017. https://ijnet.org/en/blog/women-take-lead -latin-americas-digital-media-startup-landscape.

Cabot, Heather. "How This Female Founder Took on Sexism and Raised Millions." *Forbes*, July 18, 2017. https://www.forbes.com /sites/geekgirlrising/2017/07/18/how-this -female-founder-took-on-sexism-and-raised -millions/#25c352891dfe.

Cass, Stephen. "The 2017 Top Programming Languages." IEEE Spectrum, July 18, 2017. https://spectrum.ieee.org/computing/software /the-2017-top-programming-languages.

Doyle, Alison. "Guidelines for What to Include in a Résumé." The Balance, September 16, 2017. https://www.thebalance.com/guidelines-for -what-to-include-in-a-résumé-2061035.

Doyle, Alison. "How to a Write a Résumé." The Balance, January 20, 2017. https://www .thebalance.com/how-to-write-a-resume.

Gallo, Amy. "How to Write a Cover Letter." *Harvard Business Review*, February 4, 2014. https://hbr.org/2014/02/how-to-write-a-cover-letter.

Gross, Anisse. "Women Rule in Indie Publishing." *Publisher's Weekly*, April 28, 2017. https://www.publishersweekly.com/pw/by-topic/industry-news/publisher-news/article/73469-the-indie-publishing-feminist-revolution.html.

Knowles, Rupert. "Designing for Digital Publication." Adobe Experience Manager Mobile, August 28, 2012. http://blogs.adobe.com/aemmobile/2012/08/designing-for-digital-publications.html.

Marie. "Interview with Holy from UNTOUCHD Magazine." Girls Know Tech, January 30, 2017. https://girlknowstech.com/interview-holy-untouchd-mag.

Price, Dennis. "Women-Led Digital Media Startups: Checking Corruption and Changing the Narrative in Latin America." Impact Alpha, July 21, 2017. https://news.impactalpha.com/women-led-digital-media-startups-checking-corruption-and-changing-the-narrative-fd1befe40382.

RealView Blog. "Spotlight: Women in Digital Publishing." Retrieved November 1, 2017. http://www.realviewdigital.com/spotlight-women-digital-publishing.

Skills You Need. "Interpersonal Skills." Retrieved November 1, 2017. https://www.skillsyouneed.com/interpersonal-skills.html.

Ward, Susan. "How to Be Professional." The Balance, October 27, 2016. https://www .thebalance.com/how-to-be -professional-2948360.

Wolfe, Lahle. "Digital Marketing Defined." The Balance, August 12, 2017. https://www. thebalance.com/digital-marketing -defined-3515308.

Writing Center at the University of Wisconsin -Madison, The. "Writing Cover Letters." Retrieved November 1, 2017. https://writing .wisc.edu/Handbook/CoverLetters.html.

Index

ABOUT THE AUTHOR

Hillary Dodge is a writer and librarian. She has worked with young adults for many years as a creative writing coach and community mentor. She is deeply interested in all things STEM and enjoys reading about the latest technology trends that impact libraries and publishing. You can find out more about her work and her passions at hillarydodge.com.

PHOTO CREDITS

Cover GaudiLab/Shutterstock.com; cover, interior pages (circuit board illustration) © iStockphoto.com/Vladgrin; p. 5 Squaredpixels/E+/Getty Images; p. 7 AleksandarNakic /E+/Getty Images; p. 12 Jacob Lund/Shutterstock.com; p. 13 © AP Images; p. 17 RedPixel.PL/Shutterstock.com; p. 19 © iStockphoto.com/gilaxia; p. 20 izusek/E+ /Getty Images; p. 24 Bloomberg/Getty Images; p. 27 © iStockphoto.com/georgeclerk; p. 30 Phovoir/ Shutterstock.com; p. 32 Geber86/E+/Getty Images; p. 35 Africa Studio/Shutterstock.com; p. 37 Gorodenkoff /Shutterstock.com; p. 41 gradyreese/E+/Getty Images; p. 45 © iStockphoto.com/Steve Debenport; p. 51 © iStockphoto.com/RossHelen; p. 53 stockstudioX/E+ /Getty Images; p. 55 sturti/E+/Getty Images; p. 59 Caiaimage/Sam Edwards/OJO+/Getty Images; p. 61 Rawpixel.com/Shutterstock.com; p. 64 Stuart C. Wilson /Getty Images.

Design and Layout: Nicole Russo-Duca; Editor: Rachel Aimee; Photo Researcher: Karen Huang